Praise for TOP RAN

I0019541

Scott really captures the heart and soul of search engine optimization in this guide for roofers that is just as relevant for local business in other service industries.

The story-telling writing approach makes this book 10x easier to read than alternatives that tend to read like technical documentation. There's no doubt that roofers will find the motivation they need to buy into SEO as an investment not an expense (as Scott puts it), because it focuses on the why just as much as the how, with several strategies to shape the desire for ongoing marketing efforts.

I agree with all the website recommendations and usability suggestions that support better crawler experiences, ultimately culminating into higher conversions and leads. Excellent book for local marketers and roofers alike!

Steve Wiideman, Wiideman Consulting Group

If as a roofer, you want to build perfect business, you need consistent flow of new leads to your business who want their roof fix from you, then you need get Scott Dennison's book for roofer's leads blueprint. You can implement in 1 week and starts new leads flow to your business

Muhammad Siddique, MeetSiddique.com

A great roofer with lousy marketing will get beat by an average roofer with great marketing. Scott explains in plain English how to build an online strategy to show up in Google, review sites, and social media-- then to drive more leads. If you've not tried online advertising or if it hasn't worked for you, he explains why and how to correct it. Buy this book and improve your business.

Dennis Yu, Chief Technology Officer, BlitzMetrics

Scott's book is a wonderful guide to getting noticed online and is applicable for any industry you might be in. Even if your business has been online for years, you'll probably pick up some ideas for improvements. I know I did.

Te-ge Bramhall, CompleteNovices.com

To build a real business, with high income and sustainable profits you need to have standardized repeatable processes. This is especially true for lead generation where a steady stream of new sales can allow you the freedom to create your dream business and lifestyle.

Scott Dennison knows roofing. More important, he knows the systems and methods you need to become a Top Ranked Roofer

Warren Whitlock, Influence Architect
WarrenWhitlock.com

BECOMING
TOP RANKED

A ROOFER'S GUIDE TO
DOMINATING YOUR LOCAL MARKETPLACE,
OUTSELLING YOUR COMPETITION
AND
ACHIEVING YOUR DREAM LIFE

SCOTT A. DENNISON

BECOMING TOP RANKED

A Roofer's Guide to Dominating Your Local Marketplace, Outselling Your Competition and Achieving Your Dream Life

© 2016 Scott A. Dennison

http://TopRankedRoofer.com

ISBN: 978-1-934275-11-5

Table of Contents

Foreword 1

Introduction 7
   Joe's Approach 8
   John's Approach 9
   Jack's Approach 10

The Big Promise 15
   Becoming the Top-Ranked Roofer 16
   What is Your Ultimate Outcome? 18
   Case Study –The Importance of Trust 20
   Exercise 25

Barriers on the Road to Success 29
   Barriers 30
      Time 30
      Inclination 30
      Money 31
      Skills 31
      Skilled Partners 32

The Big Problem 37
   Lack of Visibility 39
   Lack of Positioning / Lack of Uniqueness 41
   Exercise 41
      Be Unique 42
   The Importance of a Good Story 44
   Lack of Reviews and Referrals 45

Lack of Commitment / Disempowering Beliefs 46
Lack of Analytics/Tracking................................ 47
The Roofer's Biggest Enemy.............................. 48
More Problems with Roofers' Marketing 49
    Lack of Viable Solutions.................................... 49
    Generalists Versus Specialists......................... 50
    Big Companies with Evil Intent 50
    Foreign Workers 50
Story: The Roofer's Biggest Enemy..................... 52

The Big Solution 57
    What to Avoid 57
    How to Get There 58
        Enjoy Your Spot at the Top! 58
    Properly Setting up Your Google Account........... 58
        Set up a Gmail Address.................................... 59
        Google Console 59
        Google Analytics 59
        Google AdWords 60
        Summary 60
    Determine your Call to Action........................... 61
    Exercise... 61
        Communicate Your Uniqueness 63

The Three Pillars...69
    Leads in a Week... 69
        Keywords.. 70
        Landing Pages 74
    Case Study – Using AdWords............................ 76
    The Domination Springboard............................ 78
        Custom WordPress Website............................. 79
        Quality Content 80
        Google's Goals 80
        Adding Client Pictures 82
        Gathering Testimonials and Reviews 83
        Setting up Social Accounts............................. 84

Maximizing Speed 84
Exercise 85
    Mobile Readiness Test 85
    Site Speed Test 85
On Page Optimization 86
    Optimized Call to Action 86
Marketplace Domination 88
    Domain Authority 91
    Reviews – Social Proof 93

The Road to Becoming a Top-Ranked Roofer 99
    Next Steps 102
    Final Thoughts 106

Glossary 109
    Terms specific to this book 109
    Glossary of Marketing Terms 112

Acknowledgements 117

About the Author 119

Resources 121

This book is dedicated to roofers worldwide who identify with John and want, badly, to be more like Jack. My goal is to give you the tools and inspiration to take steps, everyday, to achieve your Ultimate Outcomes in life.

Foreword

I have known Scott Dennison for almost 20 years. We share many mentors; however, there is one who profoundly affected both of our business lives. His name is *Jim Rohn* and he has shared many quotes that can inspire you to run a more profitable business. When I think about the information that is contained in this book, the one quote from Mr. Rohn that jumps out is: ***"Sales is a numbers game, what one lacks in skill they can make up in numbers."*** For many years Scott and I lived by this phrase and worked harder and harder to create business revenue.

What I find great about this book is that Scott is finally and effectively addressing a topic that anyone and everyone in the roofing business absolutely needs. They need the skill to generate leads. The market is so full of contractors, both local contractors and those who quickly set up shop to take advantage of a weather pattern, that it is no longer enough to simply do the "numbers" when trying to generate new leads for roofing work. We must improve our skills to build our business. Whether you find your business currently is most aligned with Joe, John or Jack, as introduced in this book, you now hold in your hand exactly what you need to drive more leads into your business.

I work as a sales consultant with roofing contractors all over the world. Generating more leads is the key to those who are successful. Not generating leads is like a "death sentence". Having more people see and contact your company allows you to not only increase sales revenue, but also affords you the opportunity to attract the best estimators in the business to work for you. It also provides you with the chance to be selective in the jobs you accept and in the areas you work.

In this book, Scott has also tapped into the best way for contractors to decrease their cash advertising spending. Think about it: every lead you are able to generate through the proper management of your digital market presence is one that you don't have to pay for using traditional advertising methods. Consider where the next generations are going to make a decision about their home improvements.

If you want to grow your business, develop a lower cost per lead and ensure the future success of your company, then do not put this book down. This book does not belong on your bookshelf; it is not meant to be tossed aside. It requires thorough reading and you have to follow the step-by-step processes outlined in the book. This practical guide puts a plan forward, which is exactly what you'll need to know to move your business to the next level and achieve the "dream life" that Scott is promising. This will work, and it is presented in a manner that is so simple to follow that you won't even need to ask your fourteen year-old to help you like you often do when it comes to technology. There are hundreds of organizations in the home improvement industry that have and continue to apply these strategies and are reaping the benefits on their business.

Best of success!

Ron Marks
Author: Managing for Sales Results
Published by John Wiley and Sons
Phoenix, Arizona
May 2016

CHAPTER 1

Introduction

In this chapter:
- *Joe's Approach*
- *John's Approach*
- *Jack's Approach*

I don't like to generalize, but if I were to try to categorize the roofing contractors I've met, I'd say that there are three kinds of roofers.

It's a safe bet that you've met all three. You see them in the marketplace almost everywhere you go. The three roofers I detail here aren't real, but they are composites based on real people in the industry.

It's also a safe bet to say that you are one of these three roofers.

Let me run through them and see which you identify with most.

There's the guy with a pick-up truck and a ladder; he is a handyman who has done some roofing work. I'll refer to him as Joe.

Next, we have a roofer I'll refer to as John. John's been in the roofing business for a long time, and he

is a very good technician. If you have a leak, he'll
fix it. He's really good. But John's a roofer and is
still trying to find his way in business. His business
is about the same today as it was this time last
year.

He's a hard worker (when he's got a job to do) but
doesn't have a business reputation that's growing
yet, so he's struggling to achieve all that he dreams
of. His phone doesn't ring enough.

The third roofer is a man we'll refer to as Jack. He
happens to be in the roofing business, but what
really matters is that Jack's a businessman.

It doesn't seem to matter what Jack is selling, he's
a guy who understands business and understands
how to connect consumers with products and profit
from that.

Each of these roofers has a different business
approach, so let's look a bit closer at each.

Joe's Approach

Joe's approach is to drive around the neighborhood
with his pick-up truck and his ladder, stopping to
ask people he sees if they need help with anything.

He's got a magnetic sign on the side of his truck. If
he drives long enough, he's sure he can find some
people to sell something to. Maybe it's even roofing
work. It might be somebody with a leak or maybe

some loose shingles. Perhaps he meets someone on his travels who wants some trees trimmed. Joe figures, "What the heck, I've got the tools and the time, so I can do it."

But if he doesn't get a job today, he's just as happy to spend his time in the bar or coffee shop, whining that the economy is bad and there's no business.

Joe is not really a serious roofer. Joe is more of a guy who just needs to make a few bucks, and this typifies his approach to life and business.

While it was my intent to introduce you to all three roofers, this book was written for the Johns and the Jacks.

John's Approach

John is probably in the top 20% of his industry. He knows a ton about roofing, probably more than 10 roofers combined. He is good at what he does and he can find any leak and fix it.

Where John is trying to make the next leap is to move away from being a great technician and evolve into becoming a little bit more of a businessman. Instead of being a roofer, John wishes he were more of a marketing guy, kind of like Jack.

John is very much aware of Jack. He sees the guy's advertising everywhere he goes; he sees that Jack's crews have nicer trucks and equipment than he does. His company is also quite visible within the community, helping kids, sponsoring the Little League – that kind of thing.

John knows who Jack is, he's actually met him, and he is really interested in being a Jack. But he's not there yet. He has a lot to learn.

Jack's Approach

Now, if you got to spend some time with Jack, you'd realize that Jack is a businessman, and he's marketing everywhere he goes.

He's not so much in the roofing business as he is a business owner who also sells roofing. He understands that every dollar that comes in has to be tied to some form of advertising budget. Jack's met and talked to the marketing experts who try to sell him on their services, but just doesn't buy the idea that things like SEO are free.

One of the big differences between John and Jack is that Jack has a marketing budget. John just spends whatever he has in his pocket, when he has it, and sometimes he simply doesn't have it. Therefore, he is not growing nearly as effectively as Jack is.

Jack is the consummate professional. He's involved with ongoing training. He interacts with the supply houses, and he's very familiar with the companies that manufacture materials in his industry: he spends time with them. And perhaps even more importantly, because Jack is a businessman, he surrounds himself with other businessmen.

He is involved in mastermind groups of people that are as or even more successful than he is, and one of the reasons he does this is because he sees that there is an even brighter future in store for his business, even if he's come a long way from where he started.

Jack still sees opportunity to grow. So he surrounds himself with smarter people, pushing for the goal, and he knows what the goal is.

That's another big difference between Jack and John. John is selling roofing so he can make a living. He's got kids to put through school, a family to feed and a house to pay for, much like the rest of us.

On the other hand, Jack is always out marketing. He's surrounding himself with smarter people. He's always growing. He's never sitting back.

CHAPTER 2

The Big Promise

In this chapter:
- *Becoming the Top-Ranked Roofer*
- *What is Your Ultimate Outcome?*

Out on the road today,
I saw a Deadhead[1] sticker on a Cadillac.
A little voice inside my head said,
"Don't look back, you can never look back."[2]

That didn't actually happen.

I was listening to the radio when I heard these lyrics, but it made me think of something that I wanted to share with you.

What I'd like to share with you is the fact that many, many business owners are stuck. They're stuck looking back. They're wishing marketing and

---

[1] A name given to fans of the psychedelic rock band, The Grateful Dead, whose career spanned the 1960s, 1970s, and 1980s.

[2] Lyrics from a song released in 1984 by Eagles vocalist and drummer, Don Henley.

15

sales were as easy as they used to be. Maybe you are this person.

Marketing was easy in the days before market fragmentation, when there were only a few channels and you could blast a message out and those who needed your product or service would respond.

Now, we have 50,000 channels, but the problem is that audiences are very narrow and harder to reach.

Sales were easy then, too. Think back to the days before the Internet, when a yellow page ad or a print ad was all you needed to keep the phone ringing.

Compared to the old days of print and phone advertising, using the Internet to advertise requires a learning curve steeper than most we've ever had to climb and one in which bandits are hiding everywhere, waiting for their chance to steal your sack of coins.

All of these issues become history when you take a step forward and position yourself differently. Better. As the top-ranked roofer.

Becoming the Top-Ranked Roofer

Later on in this book we'll talk about a concept I created call the *triple optimization* of your business website. It's the heart of what you'll learn in this book.

It's also the secret to being the top-ranked roofer in your market. For now, I just want you to consider that whoever the top-ranked roofer is now, they are highly visible in search engines.

When a consumer with a roofing issue goes into Google to search for a roofer, the 800 lb gorilla of a roofer in your area is usually easy to spot.

He dominates Google AdWords and his ad appears at the top spot on the search page.

He has things optimized in local search, both on the website and on the related social media sites like Google+.

He also has a process in place for getting positive reviews, so he is constantly adding proof of his company's excellence for others to see. As a result, his business appears on the map on the first page of the search results.

And of course, when you finally scroll down the page to the organic lists (the 10 blue links), his site is one of the first on this list, if not at the very top of the list, as the number one roofer.

When you do all three of those things, you'll transition from being invisible on Google to being the top-ranked roofer. And that's going to make your phone ring. That's going to get you a lot more leads, and obviously, if your sales team is able to close those deals, more leads usually equals more sales, more revenues and more profits. Perhaps most importantly, the door swings open for you to achieve your Ultimate Outcomes in both business and life.

If you were the top-ranked roofer in your area, I'd be asking you, "What are you going to do with the money?"

What is Your Ultimate Outcome?

I think you'd agree that most roofing contractors don't exactly jump out of bed every day because they want to go out and put another roof on. Even if they're really good at it, even if they make a lot of money doing it, the reason that they're doing it is because there's something they want to accomplish in their life.

But, what about you?

Maybe you want to buy a new boat, maybe you want to join the country club, or maybe you want to put your kid through a private school or through college.

Maybe you need to cover insurance payments. I know one contractor who told me, "My mother is sick and the insurance doesn't cover her. I have to do this. I have to pay for this."

18

Being the top-ranked roofer, the roofer whose marketing dominates the local market, opens the door to a lot of those things. The simple truth is that when you have more sales, you'll have more profits.

Imagine if you will, deciding that you wanted to go skydiving. You know, just for fun. But not just any old skydiving will do for you. No.

You choose to go halo skydiving at 30,000 feet. This just happens to be the cruising altitude of a jet airplane. And less than 100 civilians had ever done this when two of my business partners jumped from such an airplane for such a dive.

If you were online in the mid-late 2000's, the names Yanik Silver and Mike Filsaime will probably be familiar to you. These marketing experts were the first to license some software my team and I created to sell to their followers.

Yanik and Mike were not only enormously successful in their businesses, they lived adventures that few could afford, or even imagine. These adventures included a halo skydiving adventure.

Why am I telling you this? The answer is easy. One of the biggest reasons for you to push through the challenges of entrepreneurship is because in the process, you earn the right to some adventures of your own. So you can decide on and then achieve your Ultimate Outcomes.

Case Study –The Importance of Trust

You've probably already figured out that this process for becoming the top-ranked roofer didn't just happen. Instead, it required clients with a large dose of patience and a willingness to invest in the growth of their business. However, far more important than that was their desire to trust me – the sense that I really was going to be able to help them accomplish more of their goals.

One of my clients has been working with me for almost three years now. However, when we started his project, he was completely invisible on Google. As a result, the majority of calls he got came from his listings in BBB[3] or Angie's List[4]. On occasion, an insurance adjuster would call with a lead, or the roofer's yard signs produced a call. But his business was not growing. He wanted (and needed) more leads if he

---

[3] The Better Business Bureau (BBB), founded in 1912, is a non-profit organization focused on advancing marketplace trust, consisting of 112 independently incorporated local BBB organizations in the United States.

[4] Angie's List is a US-based, paid subscription supported website containing crowd-sourced reviews of local businesses.

wanted to grow his top line revenue and bottom line profits.

It's worth noting that it wasn't due to a lack of effort on his part that he was hurting. He'd previously hired two different "experts" who claimed to be able to help him get more business from the Internet.

As I started to look for the starting point in the project, I found that both of these service providers knew less than nothing about how to make a site rank in Google, or any other search engine, for that matter.

For example, critical elements of the site itself had to be completely redone. We had a whole to-do list:

- Write new title tags
- Connect content and pages with keywords they hoped to rank for
- Address site speed
- Check what was indexed in search engines

Case Study – The Importance of Trust

Case Study – The Importance of Trust

The advanced part of all client work we do starts as soon as the site itself is fully optimized and aligns with what Google wants from you if you'd like them to rank your site well in your area.

The power of what we were doing is evident in these two contrasting images. This "before" image was generated about three months after we started working on the project.

Ranking before

Ranking Overview	8	6
0 pages ranked in position 1	0	0
2 pages ranked in position 2 – 5	2	0
8 pages ranked in position 6 – 10	8	0
14 pages ranked in position 11 – 20	14	0
14 pages ranked in position 21 – 50	14	0
13 pages ranked in position 51 – 100	13	0

Ranking after

Search engine	Top 1	In top 10	In top 100	Not in top 100
G Google	22 (+14)	30 (+17)	80 (+22)	12
G Google.com (Maps)	4 (+3)	28 (+19)	39 (+22)	53
b Bing US	19 (+17)	37 (+28)	88 (+27)	4

A total of **95** keywords are ranked on page one (the top 10) of the Google and Bing search results, with 45 of these in the prized **#1 position**, and 68 keywords listed in the most visible top three positions.

Take another look at the "before" image. You'll see that there is massive progress in keyword ranking for this site. It went from **zero** keywords ranked at #1 to 25 keywords. The keyword ranking went from 10 keywords ranked on page one of Google and Bing to 95 keywords ranked on the first page of the search results.

However, my client's real goal was to generate leads from his website. His initial goal was for us to generate 22 additional leads from his website each month. So how did we do?

Case Study – The Importance of Trust

23

Case Study – The Importance of Trust

As of the time of this writing, the client has received almost 2,000 phone calls, and 583 lead generation forms have been submitted on his website. These are exclusively his – not like those lead generation services that take a lead and offer it up to several local contractors at the same time, forcing everyone to cut prices to win the sale.

What is even more important is that more than 1,060 (41%) of these homeowners were inquiring about completely re-roofing their home.

Furthermore, 64% of the callers to his main phone number referenced Google as their source. This is what it's like to dominate your marketplace as a top-ranked roofer.

My question for you as I close this section is this: What would your business and your life look like if you had over 1,000 new, exclusive roof replacement leads and thousands of paying customers calling you in need of roof repairs?

Exercise

Grab a sheet of paper and write down one thing in your life that you know would be different if you were the top-ranked roofer!

CHAPTER 3

Barriers on the Road to Success

In this chapter:
- *Barriers:*
  - *Time*
  - *Inclination*
  - *Money*
  - *Skills*
  - *Skilled Partners*

Take a few moments to think about how your life would change if you became the top-ranked roofer in your market. Now I have a few questions for you.

Is your vision compelling? Does the thought of it energize you? I hope so, because the road ahead is filled with challenges! Many times, those challenges become barriers to your success.

I'm going to challenge you and even make myself available to help you to overcome anything that would prevent you from living your dream. But before we get to that, let's look at a few of those barriers up close.

Barriers

Time

Over the last eight years of working with business owners to tackle online marketing, the number one excuse I get for not doing what is necessary is, "I don't have time." Time (or a perceived lack of time) is not a valid reason for lack of success.

The reason is that we – and by we, I mean you, me, us – everyone from the Pope to the President to every contractor in between - have exactly the same amount of time available to us each day. How we allocate our time is what differentiates one contractor from the other. So time is not a valid excuse. But if your time is maxed out and you still want to reap the rewards of having top-ranked roofer status, know that we offer a full service option that guarantees results in writing. We'll get back to this later.

Inclination

This barrier probably applies to you more if you've been in roofing for a while, because you're probably good at what you do, especially if you're a John. What I mean by this is that you're probably aware of your strengths and also your weaknesses.

So if you've never done online marketing before, you might feel that the learning curve is insurmountable and you've come to the conclusion that you really don't want to learn how to do the marketing yourself. When you find a suitably skilled partner who you can trust to get you the results you need, then you can begin your climb to the top, without having to learn everything yourself.

Money

This can be a legitimate barrier for some roofing contractors, but for most, it's only another excuse to not jump to action. If, for example, you were to participate in the Top Ranked Roofer community (to visit the website, go to: http://toprankedroofer.com/join/), the membership fees are so low that no real businessperson could honestly say that it's too expensive.

If you choose to look closer at our full service offering, you are guaranteed a minimum ROI of $3/1. This means that, yes, you need to invest on the front end, but once the guarantee is in effect, the machine we're building together will produce a huge increase in your sales, and thus, in your profits.

Skills

A lack of skills is the most valid of all the reasons I see for not becoming the top-ranked roofer. Similar to what we said about inclination, a lack of confidence in your ability to do the work yourself is a very real barrier to success. But it should not prevent you from realizing your dream. After having worked with many business leaders on their marketing, we've learned that eight to ten steps in our *marketplace domination* program are difficult to do yourself. The good news is that we've developed a series of à la Carte services that Top Ranked Roofer community members can access at rock-bottom prices. If it's too hard for you to do yourself, a member of my team will do it for you.

Skilled Partners

A few years ago I might have considered this to be more of a challenge for a number of reasons. For one, five to ten years ago, Internet marketing wasn't all that important. If you used your nephew's friend from high school to build your website, you could get by.

That's no longer the case. According to Roofing Contractor Magazine (to visit the website, go to: http://www.roofingmagazine.com/), your online presence is a factor in 80-90% of the roofing jobs today. If your site doesn't serve the needs of searchers, Google won't even show it to your prospective customers. It's that important.

Another challenge in finding skilled partners is that you have to sort through all the solicitations you receive. Does your email get filled up with people promising you "Page One of Google?" Are a measurable number of the calls coming into your office from people trying to sell to you, rather than buy from you? How about foot traffic through your door?

There is no shortage of people offering solutions to your biggest problems, but I can save you a ton of time on all of it. If they have to press really hard to sell you, then they're not positioned well enough to attract your business. And in almost every case, you'll be dealing with someone who's got limited proof that what they do even works.

CHAPTER 4

The Big Problem

In this chapter:
- *Lack of Visibility*
- *Lack of Positioning / Lack of Uniqueness*
- *The Importance of a Good Story*
- *Lack of Reviews and Referrals*
- *Lack of Commitment / Disempowering Beliefs*
- *Lack of Analytics/Tracking*
- *More Problems with Roofers' Marketing*

I f you're clear on your Ultimate Outcome and you've dealt with the issues that come up along the way (time, money, skills, etc.), there are still several big hurdles for you to overcome on your way to becoming the top-ranked roofer.

For example, it may have already occurred to you, but Google is making this harder than it needs to be.

Why?

I can think of several reasons (I'll talk more about this later), but one is that their goals are different from yours. Google is ONLY interested in the search results of their customer, who we will define as a person who searches online using Google.

You and I would like to be found at the top of the search results, but Google isn't concerned with that. All they are concerned about is that the searchers are happy with the results they find when searching.

Take a look at your marketing campaign.

- Are you prominently visible across all the search engines?

- Are you visible on all the local forms of media that reach your neighbors in the areas that you want?

- Have you worked through the kinds of questions that you want to ask people and that you want them to ask you?

- Is your campaign built around effective communication?

This list of questions hints at some of the many things that prevent other roofing contractors from becoming the top-ranked roofers in their area.

The following sections cover a few of the other prominent issues.

Lack of Visibility

As much as it should be obvious, two things have to happen before you can make a sale. The first is that your prospects must know, like and trust you – if they don't, they won't do business with you.

For any of that to take place, they have to find you. This means that you must be visible in the marketplace.

Do you remember a song from Patsy Cline called "Crazy"? I'm dating myself now, because she released the song in 1961, before I was even born. The lyrics, in part, went like this:

Crazy, I'm crazy for feeling so lonely
I'm crazy, crazy for feeling so blue
I'm crazy for trying and crazy for crying
And I'm crazy for loving you
Crazy for thinking that my love could hold you
I'm crazy for trying and crazy for crying
And I'm crazy for loving you.

Do you know (or remember) the lyrics?

I heard the song again recently, and it got me to thinking about how these lyrics could be about the marketing some businesses do to gain visibility.

Here's an example.

Let's start with a marketing model that was popular around the time this song was in vogue - phone book advertising.

For the last 10 years or so it's been crazy to invest in display ads in the phone book.

Especially since almost everyone throws it away as soon as it gets delivered. If you do spend your marketing dollars there, you're probably feeling lonely and blue too.

Another crazy marketing model is newspaper advertising.

Most of the print media ad reps will tell you that for it to work effectively you need to run the ad over and over again. And even if it can't actually generate a measurable ROI, it gets your name out there.

I'm not saying that these models don't work, because there is a time and place when they do work. What I am saying is that today, in 2016, Roofing Contractor Magazine (to visit the website, go to: http://www.roofingmagazine.com/) tells us that 80-90% of roofing jobs start with an Internet search. If one of your problems is a lack of visibility online, start there.

Exercise

Before we take another step on this journey, let's take a minute to find out exactly where you are right now.

If you would like a free ranking report, go to: http://toprankedroofer.com/free-ranking-report-request/ and fill out the online form. You are under no obligations. It is my gift to you. Within two business days we'll send you a list showing you exactly where you rank right now in Google, for free. We'll include the keywords you rank for, the position you rank in and how much the AdWords PPC (pay per click) costs are for those keywords.

The following sections discuss a few other things your marketing may be missing.

Lack of Positioning / Lack of Uniqueness

These two items are on opposite sides of the same coin, but if you miss either of these, it will cost you a lot in sales (and revenue from those sales).

Be Unique

If you're going to become the top-ranked roofer in your market, you need to find something that makes you stand out from all the other roofers. How are you doing now? Look at 10 random roofing websites.

What words do they do to describe themselves? Most of their websites start with these words: Me, my or we.

Do your own search and here's a sample of what you'll see:

- We've been in business for 20 years.

- We are A-rated with the Better Business Bureau.

- We are an Angie's List Superior Service Award Winner.

- We've done this.

- We've done that.

What conclusion do you think the consumer comes to when reading these statements? That all these roofers are the same!

How does the consumer end up deciding on a roofing company? Probably with this thought, "Since they're all qualified, which of these roofing guys will be able to solve my roofing problem for the least amount of money?"

I was thinking about this recently when I attended a networking event near my home. Think about the last time you went to one of these. Here's what the conversation probably sounded like:

"Hi. I'm Scott. What's your name, and what do you do?"

"I'm John, and I sell promotional products and printing. We offer quality products at the lowest prices."

"Me, too."

Here's another conversation:

"Hi. I'm Jeff and I'm in roofing. We use nothing but quality roofing products and all of our materials and workmanship meets or exceeds local codes."

"Same here."

Or another conversation:

"Hi. I'm Joe and I'm a cosmetic dentist. We offer the highest quality treatments and technologies and combine the best of art and science."

"That's what I do, too."

And yet another one:

"I'm William and I'm a chiropractor. We treat families and auto accident injuries. We always use the most effective and familiar chiropractic techniques."

"Me too."

Do you see a pattern here? I got all of these conversations by looking at the top sites in each category. I found that over and over, people all say the same things about their business that their competitors do.

When this happens and all the prospect can see is that your business is no different than the other companies that do what you do, guess what? They want to decide who to do business with based on price.

Ouch!

The Importance of a Good Story

The first thing a business needs if they don't want to constantly be beaten down on their price is a unique story. They need to be able to say some things about themselves and present themselves differently than the other roofers, so that when the consumer reads all the sites, which they frequently will, they've got yours picked out as different and better. Another name for this story-telling is *positioning*.

When you take the time to position your business as better, faster or unique in some way, you have the opportunity to stand out in a crowded field of competitors.

One way to stand out as different and better is to think about a personal passion you have, and use that in your story. Chances are you're the only roofer in your area that can say something like that about yourself. Essentially it's all about having something to say that the consumer hasn't already heard, something that is different and better. It makes you stand out and it allows you to consistently get a higher price, too.

Lack of Reviews and Referrals

Even after you get your story worked out and refined, and even after you're sure that prospects will know that you are different and better than your competitors, your prospects still won't buy from you without proof that you really are better.

Your customers don't care that much about what you say about yourself. What they do care about (a lot) is what your past customers say about you.

To thrive in this competitive landscape, you'll not only have to deliver a great service, but you'll have to get good at gathering customer testimonials and reviews.

45

Much like closing sales, the key to getting reviews (and referrals) is to ask for them. But if you don't ask for a review, your customer will forget to do it. If you don't ask for any referrals, you won't get them either.

Lack of Commitment / Disempowering Beliefs

A conversation I have with nearly every client at some point, starts like this:

"Give me $20."

The reply I get the most often is, "WHY?"

"Because if you give me $20, I'll give you $100 back."

"What?!"

Now if this scene played out in reality between you and me, would you quickly pony up the money?

And if I then did follow through and immediately gave you back $100, what would your next thought be? To give me another $20, right?

With luck, you'd be allowed to continue giving me $20s and I'd continue to give you back $100s. If that were the case would you ever want to stop handing me $20s?

My point is simple. Regardless of what you've been told over the years, marketing is NOT an expense! It IS an investment.

If you can look into your past and think of a time when times got tight and you cut your marketing budget, then you'll understand what I'm talking about.

If your marketing is working and it's producing a reasonable return on the investment you're making, then you might want to consider spending more on your marketing than your competitors are.

Lack of Analytics/Tracking

One of the easiest ways to spot someone who's struggling to make their Internet marketing work for them is to check for the presence of Google Analytics or a similar tracking code installed on their site.

While I'd easily admit that Google does make it sort of complicated to use, the learning curve is worth it. It will help you solve the thorny issues around your online marketing.

According to Google, only about 50% of all websites in existence today use the free Analytics software to keep track of things on your site.

It is essential to keep track of which keywords are sending traffic to your site, how long visitors stay, which pages visitors like and which they don't.

If you lack the software or just neglect to do it, chances are you're struggling to find success with your marketing.

The Roofer's Biggest Enemy

What I've been describing all along is the list of things that roofers don't know that they don't know. When you're operating in a place where you don't know what you don't know, how can you possibly figure out what to do to change?

Think about the last time you were talking to somebody who said that they're an expert at something.

Since you've built your living on being a roofer, when somebody's telling you something about roofing, you'll know pretty fast whether or not they know what they're talking about, right?

If you've spent your entire life in roofing, or even as a business owner like Jack, there is a really good chance that when your expert starts talking about all kinds of things related to the marketing of your site, they may sound knowledgeable, but you may not have the tools to discern whether or not they are telling the truth.

If you don't know what you don't know, you can't possibly figure out what questions need to be answered before you make a commitment.

More Problems with Roofers' Marketing

Just when you think we've exhausted the list of reasons that make it difficult to market better than your competitors, we have a few more.

Lack of Viable Solutions

Since 2012, Google has changed the way they rank sites in their search results several times over. In fact, on average there's one minor change per day in how Google works. This means that the number of solutions that actually works is pretty low, and generally priced in a way that's out of reach of most companies.

Lack of Skilled Workers

Once you decide that hiring an advertising agency that says they're digital is out of reach, you may try to respond to some of those emails you've received over the years for an "expert". These are the folks who promise to get you to page one of Google, but usually they don't (or can't).

Since there are no educational requirements needed to call yourself an SEO expert, the only way to protect yourself is to do business with someone

49

you have seen over and over again – or who can prove they can deliver the results you want to achieve.

Generalists Versus Specialists

Should you find someone who you feel is skilled enough to help you, you'll want to note that most of them are generalists. This means that they will help any business owner, in any industry that can pay them.

Finding someone who has the skills you require and is a specialist in the roofing industry should be your first choice, if possible.

Big Companies with Evil Intent

One way that many roofers get hurt is to hire a big company that identifies itself as a digital marketing expert. It's very common for big old companies (like the yellow pages guys) to tell people they are now Internet marketing professionals.

Foreign Workers

This one can be a problem, but in some cases it's not. I'm talking about those who contact you, usually by email, and you can tell by the words they use that English is not their first language.

This isn't necessarily a problem. The problem lies in the fact that there is a significant difference between how Americans communicate with one another and how other cultures communicate.

If your foreign worker doesn't fully understand what you're asking for, or if they simply do the work wrong, your site can be penalized or shut down completely.

And the person who lives on the other side of the world may not know how to reverse the damage they've caused you. And they're not likely to stand behind you to solve the problem either.

Story: The Roofer's Biggest Enemy

I remember it like it was yesterday. It was a Tuesday and I was cleaning up some email when I read this:

"I've been approached many times by people offering to help with my site and I've tried several times; it never works out for me." It was an email from a roofer in California who had been reading my posts on LinkedIn.

He went on to tell me, "Recently I hired a BIG company to build my new site and generate leads for me but I didn't get even one lead. I would have done just as well to throw my money down the toilet."

As I processed what I was hearing, I almost lost it! A feeling of sickness and then anger swept over me when I understood how one company was totally abused by a major American corporation.

There's absolutely no excuse for a hard-working person to get ripped off again and again while trying to build his business. Perhaps you know someone who's also been made to suffer like this. Perhaps it's even happened to you.

And even though I have a limited capacity and can only realistically serve a small percentage of all roofers who want help, I want to scream every time I hear one of these stories.

Think about it. A well designed and constructed website requires a reasonable cash commitment. Once your website is up and running, you need to find a marketing partner. If this company is any good, their fees are going to be high.

If you choose a marketing company and then find you're getting ripped off, you have every right to be upset. Let me know, and we'll go after them together.

Story: The Roofer's Biggest Enemy

CHAPTER 5

The Big Solution

In this chapter:
- *Properly Setting up Your Google Account*
- *Determine your Call to Action*

A s we dive into the correct solution, I'm going to share with you the exact process we use to help roofing contractors dominate their local marketplace and become the top-ranked roofer.

However, as you continue reading, I'd like you to watch for something. They're big, they're powerful, and just applying these three tips to your business can make all the difference in how your plan works out.

What to Avoid

The number one thing for you to avoid is discussed in detail in the next section of this book, because even after you become the top-ranked roofer, if you miss this part, you'll spend your whole day dealing with issues about price and people who want you to work for free.

How to Get There

I'm also going to share with you the secrets of what Google *loves* about the websites it shows at the top of search results. That way, you can use these secrets, too. This information will help you to climb upwards in the search results until your phone rings with high-quality local roofing leads all day long. So make sure you look for it.

Enjoy Your Spot at the Top!

Finally, one of the real keys to success is being able to clearly see or visualize how your business and personal life will change as a result of being the top-ranked roofer. If you can see into the future to the point where you need new crews to keep up, you'll have an immediate source of inspiration, which is what you'll need to accomplish your vision. I've included a handy free tool toward the end of the book that will help you every step of the way.

Properly Setting up Your Google Account

The first three steps that lead up to the pillars are the foundation of the whole process. Most companies do only one of these three steps. What sets us apart is that we do the other two steps.

The first critical step that is of the foundation of your top-ranked roofing business is to make sure that you have all of the most important Google properties set up in advance. If you think about it, Google has all these tools they let us use for free – they just want us to use them.

So to set your business foundation in place, here are the accounts you want to have (at a minimum).

Set up a Gmail Address

I recommend that you set this up first, and then use the same Gmail address for every Google account. This way they're all tied together.

Google Console

This was previously named Google Webmaster Tools and is a very powerful tool for optimizing your site. In about five minutes we can see all of the sites that link to your sites, as well as the anchor text (keywords) used in linking to your site. I'll explain the importance of this a little later when we get to the section about building domain authority.

Google Analytics

Of all the essentials you need to build a strong online business, information is truly important. Analytics is another free Google tool that tells you how many visitors you've had on your site, what pages they looked at, how long they visited, and what page they were looking at when they chose to leave.

Google AdWords

The AdWords tool was created to manage your Google advertising account. The very unique *Leads in a Week* service that we offer at Top Ranked Roofer is a critical part of our program, mostly because our clients need to generate some sales to offset the investments they make in hiring us.

The AdWords tool helps us to keep track of the keywords you're advertising on, but also the ads themselves and the performance (in real time) of your advertising.

Within the tool itself you can write and test new ads, increase or decrease your budgets and even stop your advertising all together. You'll need the free AdWords tools to be able to buy advertising from Google.

Summary

You'll want to use at least the four Google services listed above. Google definitely favors those websites that use all of their stuff. If you're working with us, we'll show you what those things are, or we'll do them for you.

Exercise

Create your own Gmail account. To visit the website, go to: https://mail.google.com/. In the top right corner, choose Sign-up. Walk through the steps in sequence. When you're done, you'll have a new Gmail account to use in setting up your other Google services accounts.

Determine your Call to Action

Perhaps you've heard the expression, "A confused mind always says no." Have you ever given much thought to what that expression means?

The clearer you are in deciding what you want for your business (and your life), the easier it will be to find the path that will lead you there.

Start by asking yourself these questions:

- Do I want to be the top-ranked roofer in my area?

- Do I want my phone ringing constantly?

- Do I want more leads?

61

If you answered yes to any of these questions, then ask yourself these questions:

- Am I willing to commit to it?

- Am I willing to work for it?

- Am I willing to invest in it?

These are the questions that I would ask you, but I can't answer them for you. Only you can do that. Only you know what your real motivation is.

If you answered yes to these questions, then remember that your prospective customer is just as bedeviled with confusing decisions as you are.

Successful online marketing requires you to be crystal clear on what you want a visitor to your site to do.

As a roofer you need to know and communicate what you expect from your potential client once the client has found you and visited your site:

- Do I want the client to fill out a form?

- Do I want the client to phone me?

- Do I want the client to read a particular article?

- Do I want the client to download a certain report?

- What do I want the client to do?

The answer to these questions helps determine the focal point of your website. It dictates the placement of certain elements of your new site so that consumers understand how best to respond to your offer of solving their current roofing issue.

Communicate Your Uniqueness

Once you're really clear about the call to action, you need to clearly know who you're targeting and who your ideal customer is. You need to be able to communicate what makes you different and what makes you better.

If you've looked at as many roofing sites as I have, you will see a lot of this: "We've been in business 20 years." Or: "We've been in business 15 years, and we've got an A+ rating with the Better Business Bureau." Or: "We are an Angie's List Super Service Award winner." Or: "We have reviews from Yelp, and..."

Looking at these, you'll see that they all say pretty much the same thing. Why is this a problem? If the top 10 roofing sites all say the same thing about themselves, then the costumers are likely to think, "I don't see anything unique about these guys." If they do conclude that you're all the same, they're either going to continue their search, or they're going to start sending out requests for a quotation and start looking to see who is the cheapest.

The customer's objective becomes finding the roofer who can do the job for the least amount of money. This stems from a mistake that the business owner makes.

It isn't the consumer being cheap; it's the business owner failing to communicate all of the things that make his business is unique. It's the business owner completely missing the mark at telling prospects why they're better than everybody else.

This is definitely a step we want to spend some time on.

Clients are often shocked and surprised how quickly we can position them as a top-tier roofer who commands and receives premium pricing for their work. We have a process that we use with clients to talk to them about their niche, so that they can target the audience that they're most interested in, and then we show them how to clearly communicate that on their website. We want to make sure people know that this roofer is not like the other nine roofers. He is different. He's better.

Once you've got your foundation in place, the process moves into its next phase. With your foundation and the *Three Pillars* in place, you'll be well on your way to becoming the top-ranked roofer in your area, if only by default.

Let's have a look at each of the *Three Pillars* and then consider the strength of them combined.

CHAPTER 6

The Three Pillars

In this chapter:
- *Leads in a Week*
- *The Domination Springboard*
- *On Page Optimization*
- *Marketplace Domination*

As the saying goes, "A cord of three strands is not easily torn apart." If you think about it, there's truth to this statement.

Earlier in the book I mentioned the *triple optimization* of your business website. This is what I was referring to. If you take my advice and follow this plan to set your Internet marketing efforts up correctly and implement each of the three pillars, you'll have a solid business that can compete with anyone.

Leads in a Week

The first pillar, the one on the left, is called *Leads in a Week*. All of the roofers I know want their phone ringing - now. It's an urgent situation. Maybe you can relate.

Perhaps they don't have enough business and they are worried because payroll is coming and they've got to pay their vendors.

Our idea was to start generating leads right now, within a week.

We will, nearly simultaneously, get to work on building your site and doing all the other things that will make you a top-ranked roofer in organic search listings and in the map listings, but now, right now, we need the phone to ring with leads.

There are three parts to the *Leads in a Week* process. Let's look at all three a little closer.

Keywords

We agree that at least one of your goals is that you want to start generating leads in a week. As mentioned, the way we do that is to do some focused keyword research, and then set up the landing pages for the initial AdWords campaign.

To start, we can shorten the process of keyword research by plugging a well-established list of keywords into our favorite research tool, Market Samurai (to visit the website, go to: http://www.marketsamurai.com/).

In the roofing niche, the keywords we want to use include:

70

- Roofing (city)

- (City) roofing

- Roofer (city)

- (City) roofer

- Roofing contractor (city)

- Roofing contractors (city)

- Roofing company (city)

- Roofing companies (city)

- (City) Roofing contractor

- (City) Roofing contractors

- (City) Roofing company

- (City) Roofing companies

As you can see, the list is not very broad. This is intentional. We want to make it possible for you to advertise profitably, right out of the gate.

When you broaden the types of keywords you're advertising on (a subject too advanced for this book), you can definitely generate more traffic to your site. You can spend more money on ads. But if you're like many others who've tried before you, you can lose a bundle on those ads and rarely make money. If you're tempted to try it, then be sure to read the case study at the end of this section.

One other thing you'll want to do in advance of setting your ads upon the world is to take your list of keywords and "wrap" them.

The tool we use is free. To download the Google Adwords Keyword Tool, go to: http://www.adwordswrapper.com/cgi-bin/aw.cgi

Simply take the list of keywords from the list above (with the city names added) and paste them into this tool.

You'll get a list of the following keywords in the section called "Phrase" & [Exact] Match:

"Roofing Denver"

"Denver roofing"
[Roofing Denver]

[Denver roofing]

The keyword in quotes is a "phrase" match. The keyword in brackets is an [exact] match. This means that your ad will only show for someone who has typed the term either in quotes or in brackets, but it will NOT show for searches where they're looking for only a part of the keyword.

If you're wondering about all this, think about it. I'm sure that you don't want to show up for people searching for a restaurant in Denver, just because your ad has the city name in it.

One other critical safeguard to your *Leads in a Week* process is to enter negative keywords. These tell Google to NOT display your ad when someone searches for these types of words.

Here's a list of some negative keywords:

- career
- careers
- employment
- hiring
- intern
- interns

While there are thousands of potential negative keywords you might want to exclude, it's easy to understand why you wouldn't want your ad to show up for searches like this.

Once you've selected your keywords and your keywords are wrapped, the next step is to develop a landing page for your campaign.

Landing Pages

When clients trust us to implement the *Leads in a Week* service for them, we don't start without building a custom landing page for their campaign.

This is a critical step, because the number one most expensive mistake that a roofer makes is trying to generate leads quickly using something like Google AdWords without using landing pages.

To help you understand, most roofers trying Google AdWords send traffic to the home page of their site.

But not you. You're an emerging top-ranked roofer. Instead of sending traffic to your main (home) page, you direct your traffic to a landing page, an internal page, which discusses exactly what the person was looking for.

For example, if the average visitor clicks on your ad because it says, "Top roofer in Denver. Get your free roofing inspection. Call now." What they will see on your landing page should answer the initial question they have about you, which is, "How can I get that free roofing inspection?" If your landing page has a clear call to action (so if it answers their question), they're probably going to contact you. This is why we use landing pages.

When your potential customers search others' ads, if there are no landing pages, they will be directed to the site's home page, where they will be looking for that specific thing that they clicked on the ad for. What was it that made them click? If they don't see it when they first get there, they're just going to hit the Back button and go on to the next guy.

As the roofer, you don't even know the customer was there, except that the customer's footprints are in your AdWords account, because Google lifted $8 or $10 or $12 (or more) out of your account because your site was visited by a hot prospect.

And Google doesn't care that you didn't close the deal. They generated the lead, but you didn't close the deal.

Our *Leads in a Week* service is a serious play – it can take a roofing contractor with only a tiny amount of business and fill his pipeline with leads starting right away.

Case Study – Using AdWords

I have a client in Houston, Texas. He is a roofing contractor who has been in business for 25 years. When I met him originally, he was hemorrhaging from Google AdWords. He was being slaughtered by it. And he couldn't really tell me what was going on, other than, "It's not working," and, "It's driving me down the tube financially."

I was trying to explain that if you use Google AdWords properly, it is the easiest, fastest, most profitable way to get visitors to your site. But you have to do it right; you can't just throw something together. So I looked at what he was doing. First of all, he was sending traffic to the home page of his website.

The vast majority of people are looking for something specific, and he sent them to something general. So they all left without buying anything.

We looked at his account and we found that he was paying about $40 per click. A lot of people who have never done AdWords will struggle to understand this. Your ad is running on Google and it doesn't cost you anything to just sit there.

76

However, if someone clicks on your ad and goes to wherever the link takes them, Google will charge you for whatever the current bid for that keyword is. It could be $6, it could be $10, and it could be $40. It changes constantly because it's a live auction, and it's moving all the time. So he was paying about $40 for each roofing click, and it was taking him about 15 clicks to get one bona fide sale. So this guy was spending $40 times 15, or $600, to generate one sale. The cost of sales was way too high. It wasn't sustainable.

If your lead gets you a roof repair that generates $300 and it costs you $600 to generate the repair, it's not worth it. Obviously, if you sell nothing but new roofs, you could make that up, but it still cuts into your margins tremendously.

What we ended up doing was to analyze everything that was going on. First we put up a landing page, two of them, actually, and we started creating tighter ad campaigns with a narrow focus, and we sent potential clients to these landing pages. Within two weeks, his costs had dropped to $12 a click from $40.

Case Study – Using AdWords

Case Study – Using AdWords

The most important thing was that it has gone from 15 clicks to about three or four clicks to make a sale. So his cost per sale dropped down to around $40 to $50 from $600.

If you roll those numbers out over a period of several months, you can see how having someone who knows what they're doing is very inexpensive compared to what it's costing you to do things improperly.

This *Leads in a week* piece is a major part of what we do, because what it does is allows the guy to get his phone ringing and start benefitting from the top-ranked roofer status before his website is even done.

As we discussed earlier, Leads in a Week is just one of the three pillars in the Top Ranked Roofer model for success. Let's look at the next pillar.

The Domination Springboard

If you've ever had the chance to hear me speak on this topic, or if you've read my blog, you've probably heard me refer to the *Marketplace Domination* program we offer.

When you implement all three pillars as we suggest, in just a few months you'll be positioned as the top-ranked roofer in your area. As a result, you'll dominate your marketplace.

Many aspects of your online marketing come into play in this pillar, so let's look closer at them now.

Custom WordPress Website

In this phase you want to take the information that you gathered in the call to action and the uniqueness steps, and sit down at your computer to build a custom WordPress website for your business.

I'm not sure if you've considered how hard it would be for me to describe, step-by-step, how to do that and if you doubt that it's even possible, I understand.

For that reason, I've made a short video to demonstrate the essential steps to getting your site online. To access the video, go to: http://toprankedroofer.com/bonuses/.

You can (and perhaps will) spend months or even years making improvements to your site. Your site might be fairly basic, but it will meet the needs of your audience. And you can do it in a day or less.

Once the basic website is launched, it's easy to update things to include your colors and your logo.

You want to customize your website to meet your specifications.

WordPress is based on templates, so your website will have some similarities to other sites. But what customers care about is whether or not you are unique and whether you can prove that you can solve their problem.

If the site generates leads for you, that's fantastic. If it also looks great, and it's fast and it does everything that it's supposed to do, that's even better.

Quality Content

The one thing that Google wants most is high quality content. Definitions regarding what quality actually means have been revised completely in the last five years.

Google's Goals

Google's main goal is to serve their audience, and their audience is the person who searches using Google. Everything they do is to benefit the person who searches using Google.

They don't care at all about me as a business owner. They only care that the person who is searching for something will use Google, and secondly, that this person will find what s/he's looking for. And of course the hope is that what this person finds is relevant, and of excellent quality.

To address all of the poor quality content that was being published, Google has created what is commonly referred to as their *Panda algorithm.* Panda is really little more than a math formula, but essentially, what it measures is whether or not you have quality content on your site.

Google wants to provide an excellent experience, and they want excellent content to be the driver of that experience.

Here are a few things that define the current standard of quality:

- *400 plus words per page.* Not long ago, 300 words on a page were considered adequate. Now 300 words are considered "thin".

- *No duplication of content.* The content on one page should be unique to that page and not appear on other pages of the site (or on other sites).

- *It must be readable.* You might think that this goes without saying, but the fact is that in 2012, a huge number of searches returned content that was a bunch of words arranged around a keyword, but they had no meaning.

81

- *Lack of keyword stuffing.* There once was a time when it was recommended you use your keyword (i.e. Denver roofing) in one article until its density was about 5%. This meant saying stuff like, "Western Sun, a Denver roofing company is the best Denver roofing company in the Denver area." Seriously? But it did happen, regularly. Today you can use the word one time, and as long as you also use the keyword in your page title, you've communicated to Google what this page of your site is about.

When you hire us to complete the work for you, we'll initially set up 10 pages of great content on the major parts of your business that need to be communicated. As it is your site, you can add as many pages as you prefer, but I'd shoot for at least ten.

Adding Client Pictures

Once the pages have been set up and content has been added to them, the next step is to incorporate high-quality images into your site.

Roofers have so many opportunities to take great pictures, but I hear lots of excuses about why they don't do it more regularly.

Here's what you should know. On sites I manage that have great pictures, especially before and after pictures, the gallery page is the most visited page on the site.

You can leave that out, but know that your prospective customers like pictures of your work and in fact, pictures often make them decide in favor of your business.

When you don't have pictures of jobs you've completed, it also makes it harder to prove that your work is good.

Gathering Testimonials and Reviews

I suspect you know this already, but your future customers care a lot more about what past customers have to say about your business than about all of the things you say about yourself. When we do a project for a client, we help them gather their customer testimonials and incorporate them into the website.

Once the social accounts are in place, some of them are good at facilitating the collection of reviews and testimonials. In fact, Google + (aka: Google My Business) shows your reviews on page one of search results for major keywords.

If you have enough high-quality reviews on your Google+ page, you can spring to the top of the map results in many of the smaller towns in your service area. That's not a guarantee, but I have seen it happen.

Setting up Social Accounts

Our next step is to set up all the social accounts that you need to properly get your message out. Ultimately you'll choose which ones to use, but since your customers are often homeowners, I'd start with Facebook and Twitter, and then add Google My Business and LinkedIn to round out the mix.

Yes, there are thousands of other sites, like Pinterest and Instagram for your pictures. If you have time to set them up and have time to add content to them, fine. If not, choose the ones you can manage and participate in, so that if someone contacts you through your social site, you'll be able to respond.

Maximizing Speed

One of the last things we do before we complete this phase of the project is to maximize the site's speed, because Google wants the website to be really fast. Speed is one of those things that Google monitors. With so many people using mobile phones, we went through a shakedown in 2015 that we've dubbed "mobile-geddon". Google said, "If you don't have a mobile version of your website, we're going to drop you from the search results." They've made a lot of changes like that. And if more than 50% of your searches are coming through mobile devices, you'd better be found in the mobile search or you're going to lose out on a ton of business.

Exercise

Here are two free and quick tests you can run on your site to see how you're doing on two of the things Google looks at in deciding where to rank your site.

Mobile Readiness Test

Find out if your website is mobile-ready. Go to: https://www.google.com/webmasters/tools/mobile-friendly/. Enter your business website address to see if Google considers your site as mobile friendly or not.

Site Speed Test

Find out if your website is fast enough. Go to: https://gtmetrix.com/. Enter your website address to see how fast your website loads and is visible to visitors. Ideally, your site should load in less than two seconds. When you run this test, you'll know exactly how fast your site is and you'll get a list of things you can do to speed things up.

On Page Optimization

On-page optimization of your site is the last step in the *Domination Springboard* phase of your ascent to top-ranked roofer status. The optimization you'll do includes checking the title tag, header and alt tags and the meta data to ensure that you're giving Google all it needs to be able to determine that your web page is of high-quality and gets ranked properly in search results.

I have a short video to show you how to check and improve the most important elements. To access the video, go to: http://toprankedroofer.com/bonuses/.

Optimized Call to Action

When we work with our private clients, there are about 15 steps that we take a website through, and we've laid most of them out for you here.

If you remember in the *Foundation* phase, we spent time deciding what an ideal call to action was for your business. Now we have to implement that call to action by moving it to a prominent place on the website, so nobody can miss it.

In every roofer's site we do, we list the company's phone number in the top right corner of the site, in big bold print, because that's where people will expect to find it.

We also add a banner to the middle of the home page that restates the call to action (e.g.: Request Your Free Roofing Inspection), so you can clearly communicate to all your visitors how they are supposed to respond.

And we add a form to almost every page of the site to make it easy for someone to request his or her inspection without calling and speaking to anyone. Instead, the company receives the visitor's information by email. This sets you up to call them to follow up and schedule an appointment.

Once the website is ready, we move on to the *Marketplace Domination* phase. This is an ongoing process that only needs to end when you've achieved all your goals and are ready to sell out or retire.

The good news is that results come quickly. In most projects, we start to see visible, tangible results within three to six months.

Think back to when I told you about the client who has received almost 2,000 phone calls and 600 exclusive lead generation forms on his website. Does the thought of something like that happening to you get you fired up?

In this next section, I'll tell you how my client did that and how you can go from invisible in Google to one being of the most visible roofers in your market.

The steps we need to take on the path that leads us there is to gather what is known as 'authority', that, when combined with all the other information we're communicating to Google, helps them decide that YOU are the top-ranked roofer and that you want people searching for roofing help in your area to find you.

Marketplace Domination

I'll always remember the day I was sitting with a group of entrepreneurs in a class being led by Jack Canfield and Mark Victor Hansen.

Even if their names don't ring a bell, I'm sure you've seen (or owned) some of their work. They were the authors of the *Chicken Soup for the Soul* book series.

The company started in 1993 and all these years later has published more than 250 books and sold more than 11 million copies. But in the beginning, as it is with many businesses, success wasn't guaranteed.

From arguments over the name to disagreements over the type of stories they wanted to publish, to finding a publisher, things got off to a rocky start.

Then they had their big break: An appearance on The Oprah Winfrey Show. While they were waiting backstage, a show producer walked in to tell them the timing of things and what to expect.

As he turned to go, he mentioned, "Oprah loves the book and will hold it up and show it to the audience."

Mark and Jack both thought that sounded great but didn't understand how significant such an act was. "What does that mean?" Jack asked.

The producer laughed and said, "Buy the beach house Jack, it's paid for!"

Imagine having someone say such a thing to you… no, cancel that thought. What I want you to do is walk into the nearest room with a mirror (the bathroom maybe?) and say to the person staring at you in the mirror to "Buy the beach house *insert your name here*, it's paid for!"

Because if you're willing to take the steps I've outlined up to this point, you'll be on track to achieve the biggest of your Ultimate Outcomes.

Even though we probably haven't met, I know you well enough to know that you have a dream or two that has eluded you so far.

Maybe even to the degree that you're beginning to believe it will never happen for you.

Remember the quote from football coach Vince Lombardi? "It's not whether you get knocked down; it's whether you get up."

Perhaps even better is the Japanese proverb, "Fall seven times. Stand up eight."

As we proceed to the third pillar of our top-ranked roofer model, I want to congratulate you on what you have already accomplished.

If you've implemented each of the steps as you've read through this book, you already have a much improved website that's being filled with high-value information.

Visitors to your site are clear on why you're better than the other roofers in your area and your call to action is crystal clear. This means you've already got more leads than you did just a short time ago.

You've already set up your first landing page and are getting some calls and opportunities from your *Leads in a Week* project.

Yes, if you've been following along, you're probably feeling pretty good about the decision you made to invest time and focus on this.

But there's more.

I promised you the opportunity to dominate your market and become the top-ranked roofer there, right?

From where you are currently, you already have much of what it will take to be the 800 lb. gorilla in your market.

There are just a few things missing. Get those in place and you'll enjoy some smooth sailing and your progress will be consistent.

I'm talking about gathering domain authority and social proof that you are who you say you are and that your business has a solid reputation for the work it provides.

Domain Authority

I'm not going to try to explain how search engine optimization (SEO) works. Instead, I'll just reduce it to this. Most of the formulas for where your site is ranked are based on math.

And if your site has more domain authority than the site listed ahead of you, your site will advance ahead in the search results.

In time, the accumulation of domain authority will result in you having no competitors left ahead of you in the SERPs (Search Engine Results Pages). When that happens, you'll be the top-ranked roofer.

The goal then is to build and gather an ongoing amount of domain authority. There are many ways to accomplish this goal, but there are only a few that Google actually approves of. There are many ways to gain domain authority that Google hates and will punish you for if you do any of these in your attempt to gain search engine visibility.

91

The best practices are to attract links from related sites to yours (for example, from other construction related companies) by creating high quality content that these companies would like to share with visitors to their business.

In some cases they'll add your content to their site and link to you as the source. In other cases they'll only share your content via Twitter or some other social site.

It's not important how they go about helping to promote you. What's important is that they do. Usually the best way is to ask them what their readers would benefit from, and then create something just for them.

While this book is not a link-building course, there are ways of getting links coming in to your site that can help you to accumulate some domain authority. Some of the most popular include:

- Submitting guest blog posts to other blogs

- Submitting your blog to directories listed on a website such as: http://bestoftheweb.org

- Finding directories in your niche and submitting your link for inclusion

- Interviewing (and being interviewed by) other bloggers

- Getting clients, vendors and friends to link to your site

- Making sure your social profiles (Facebook, Twitter, LinkedIn) include a link to your site

- Adding your blog to different communities by taking part in a blog carnival, where a blog owner invites other bloggers to participate and post topics on the same theme.

- Answering questions for people on sites like Quora.com (to visit the website, go to: https://www.quora.com/).

- Starting or participating in forum conversations and linking to your own site in the signature

Reviews – Social Proof

If you have been in business for even a few months, you have generated some word of mouth advertising for your work. Good or bad, people are talking.

This is good because your next customer cares a lot about what your last customer said about you. They care a whole lot more what that buyer says about you than anything you say about yourself.

I've seen research that shows that over 60% of all sales involve researching your online reputation. So if your reviews are negative, it's costing you sales. If they are positive, they are helping you to close sales.

But recently we've seen more reasons for you to want to gather testimonials and reviews and to remain focused on those testimonials with every sale.

One of my clients offers a high-end service and he's developed a solid strategy for getting those all-important reviews.

Once his total reviews reached a bit north of 50 (done over a period of years, not months), Google decided to show him on other Maps pages in his area.

His domination at getting reviews shot the company ahead in 12 other local municipalities near his offices and his phone started to ring like crazy from that.

The best way to get more reviews is to ask. It's that simple. If you ask everyone you do work for, some will say yes. Don't be concerned about the ones who say no; just focus on the yeses and you'll do fine.

One other tip I share with clients is this: getting reviews on Google+ is often very challenging, because Google is very tough on sites that post fake reviews.

They have lots of data to compare to and if they suspect that the review that was just posted is faked in some way, they'll take it down.

The easiest way to get lots of Google reviews is to pay attention to the email address the prospect gives you. If it's a Gmail address, they have a Google account and reviewing you is easy for them.

Every other type of email address should be referred to some other site to leave you a review. (such as BBB, Yelp, Facebook, etc.)

CHAPTER 7

The Road to Becoming a Top-Ranked Roofer

In this chapter:
- *Next Steps*
- *Final Thoughts*

W hat I've laid out for you in this book is a step-by-step plan, a roadmap if you will, that will lead you from being invisible in search engines to becoming the top-ranked roofer in your market.

In case I need to remind you, the roofing contractor who is perceived to be #1 will get far more calls and leads than his or her competitor. And I probably don't need to tell you that more calls and leads can mean more sales and profits for you.

As we've discussed before, this is nothing but an opportunity to contribute in your community at a greater level. That's where the real satisfaction comes in.

We covered the foundational essentials to marketing your roofing business today; things like using Google's tools wisely and thinking through your unique positioning so you're not thought of as the cheap guy in town.

We covered my *triple optimization* strategy in detail. To review, here's what you'll need to do:

- Execute on my *Leads in a Week* strategy to launch a narrowly focused AdWords effort to get your phone ringing now.

- Leverage the *Domination Springboard* to build the right type of WordPress website filled with high-quality, high-value content.

- Slowly and progressively reach *Marketplace Domination*, until your roofing business has complete visibility in local maps and listings as well as organically.

If you follow through and triple optimize your roofing business online as I've outlined, there is no telling how far you'll go.

I hate to say this, but the most common response to the plan outlined in this book is to do nothing.

This reminds me of a story. A man, while exploring his property one day, discovered that the boarded up cave in the back was actually the entrance to an abandoned gold mine.

He pulled back the boards and walked in. When he shone a light into the cave, he discovered that the mine was still filled with gold.

Quietly, day after day, he dug and filled wheelbarrows with the ore. He sifted, sorted and processed the gold into riches for himself and his family.

After some months of this he realized that there was no end to the gold in his mine, so he approached his friend and neighbor to tell him of his good fortune. More importantly, he invited his friend to get his wheelbarrow and shovel and join him in the digging.

His friend, however, did not look so happy with the proposition. He replied, "I don't have a wheelbarrow or a shovel."

The man said, "Then get one."

His friend replied, "No. They cost too much."

Done right, using a direct response approach to marketing, the process we've laid out in this book asks you to invest a dollar and get $3, $5, $10 or more dollars in return for your investment.

Some would say this is a no-brainer, while others would say, "I don't have the dollar."

Such is the life of roofing contractors and business leaders today. Some will see the opportunity to improve their marketing and will start mining for gold, while others, focused solely on what they don't have, insist that they can't afford to improve their marketing.

Which are you? I don't know, but I suspect you do.

Next Steps

We started this book by talking about the three roofers, otherwise known as Joe, John and Jack.

You may not have noticed, but little has been mentioned of Joe since the beginning. That was done on purpose, because in reality, this book was not written for him.

Joe is often blown along by circumstances and is more of a handyman than a roofer. He's therefore unlikely to apply this process to his business and achieve something great. I'd much rather focus my efforts around those who are ready for more.

John, as we mentioned earlier, is very clear of who Jack is, pays attention to much of what Jack does in his business and wants that level of success for himself.

If you, in reading this, relate to John, then there are two paths that you can follow.

The first is for you to learn more about the Top Ranked Roofer community. You might say, "What is that?" It's the only private marketing support membership community for roofers, anywhere on planet Earth.

In the Top Ranked Roofer private membership community, I'll teach you step-by-step how we build our roofing contractor client's business from invisible status, where their phone rings so rarely they wonder if it was disconnected, to a point where they have so much business, they are booked weeks and months into the future.

More important than the info you'll have access to, you'll also be invited into the private, members-only forum, where you can get feedback and help on your marketing from our experts as well as from peers who are on the same journey as you are.

Joining the Top Ranked Roofer community (to visit the website and find out more, go to: http://toprankedroofer.com/join) is so affordable that no real business could say they're unable to afford it.

The other path available to you, as a roofing contractor, and as leader of your fast-growing firm, is to choose to hire someone to help you with your marketing. If you would like a no-cost, no-obligation call with Scott A. Dennison, you can fill out a form by going to: http://toprankedroofer.com/request-call-scott/.

This is a path you may be considering. It's also something that statistically you've already done at least once before.

As I think about all of my private clients, each and every one of them had hired someone to do SEO before they started to work with me. Now, I don't actually DO SEO but since it is a tiny slice of what we do, I'll use it to make my point.

The contractors who chose to hire me to help them knew that getting more visible on Google would change things for them. In trying to hire "experts" before, they learned how to evaluate the type of work I do.

They know what value looks like.

I've been told by many of them that they understand enough of what I do to know that it's not good value for them to learn and then implement what I already do every single day.

We do offer a full lead generation service that is fully guaranteed in two ways. To learn more about working with me and my team, go to: http://toprankedroofer.com/request-call-scott/.

One day I was chatting with a new client and he was asking me to tell him why he should choose to work with me.

I asked him, "Would you try to climb Mt. Everest without an expert guide? Would you attempt to fly a balloon across the Atlantic Ocean without years of training and coaching from someone who's done it? Would you consider making your first ever shark dive with the Great White Sharks off the Great Barrier Reef without knowing the cage you're using is built for the task?"

If you said no to any or all of these, let me ask you one more question.

WHY would you try to navigate the high peaks, hurricane force winds and vicious predators that stand between you and the type of business you dream about, without expert marketing assistance?

So here's the truth: Just about every business owner who will buy and read this book is looking either for clues to help them or an expert to do it for them.

Can you relate?

If you think I've got the time or inclination to sell you on working with me, I don't. There are thousands of roofing contractors in North America, and serving the ones who ask for help keeps me busy enough to earn a full time living.

I'd be delighted to talk to you. I'll do everything I can to help you succeed. But I simply won't try to sell you on working with me.

Final Thoughts

I was reading a newsletter I get from one of my teachers the other day and he suggested that for entrepreneurs like us, OK was a 4-letter word.

Or at least it should be.

If you think about it, he's right too. Do you want to have an "OK" marriage? Do you want kids that are just "OK"? After working hard all year, will you be content with an "OK" vacation? What about an "OK" retirement? Would you be satisfied with "OK" health?

When it comes to your marketing, is it just "OK"? How about the revenues in your business, are they just "OK"?

If you ask (and answer) each of these questions of yourself, I think you may want to join me in concluding that OK is a 4-letter word. Jim Collins, author of the book "Good to Great", said that "Good is the enemy of great," and in that he's 100% correct.

The bigger question is: what do we do about it? How do we move beyond "OK" or good and go for something better? How do we go for something great?

First, we decide.

Then we plan.

Then we surround ourselves with people who can help.

Then we take action.

Reading that newsletter the other day caused me to have a conversation with a friend where I said, "With the years I've got left, I want to be in pursuit of 'spectacular'."

It's possible for me and it's possible for you. All you have to do is decide, plan, get help and act.

It's my wish for you...

Glossary

Terms specific to this book

"BS" - *aka: Belief Systems* - A number of years ago, motivational speaker Anthony Robbins was talking about belief systems and suggested that many were so strong they blocked people like you and me from success. I've often diagnosed that it was the belief that something wouldn't work and nothing that would prove that the thing wouldn't work, but that belief prevented the achievement of success. In most cases our own BS will prevent us from being top-ranked roofers, nothing more.

Domination Springboard - *Domination Springboard* represents the second and mega-critical pillar in the process of taking a roofer from where they are to being the top-ranked roofer in their community. This involves analyzing and then fixing many aspects of a roofer's website to align it with what Google wants. Fixing these things allows your site to rank among the leaders in your market. This, combined with the *Marketplace Domination* phase of the work we do

109

for private clients, positions them for top-ranked roofer status.

Domain Authority (DA) - According to an online marketing software website, MOZ (to visit the website, to go: https://moz.com/), Domain Authority is a score (on a 100-point scale) that predicts how well a website will rank on search engines. Use Domain Authority when comparing one site to another or tracking the strength of your website over time. Since it is the accumulation of DA within your site that is a major factor in where your site will rank, you can rank better when your site attracts links from other important sites.

Leads in a Week - This is our own unique process for developing and deploying hyper-local Google AdWords campaigns, doing it fast, and as a result, generating high-quality local roofing leads within a week from when we started.

Marketplace Domination - This term has two meanings within the context of this book. First, it represents the third and final pillar in the process of becoming a top-ranked roofer. Second, it represents the position our top-ranked roofers have in their local marketplace. When a roofer is highly visible everywhere that a consumer looks for a local roofer, that roofer often experiences marketplace domination, meaning their phone is ringing with opportunities, even if your competitors' phones aren't.

Optimized Call to Action - Most roofing contractors have something of a call to action; very few have their call to option optimized based on the responses of real visitors. By taking time to think through the strategy of the call to action and its placement on the page, we can often increase your lead generation results by as much as 40%.

The Three Pillars – This is the visual representation of our services and training. Implementing all three pillars is how you would *triple optimize* your roofing website, achieve visibility across the three major Google properties and become the top-ranked roofer in your area.

Triple Optimization - When a site is *Triple Optimized*, it means that you're improving your business presence in all three places that Google offers visibility to a roofing company.

1. You want to be seen in the ads at the top of most search pages. If your keyword is [City] Roofing Contractors, and you see ads at the top of the search results, you want to be seen there because you'll get lots of calls and leads from it.
2. In the map that appears just below the ads there are three roofers shown. If your company is found there, it will result in a lot of local calls.

111

3. You definitely want to be found in the organic
    listings toward the bottom of the page. Many
    people who search will look at and contact
    the companies listed on page one of Google
    search results.

Ultimate Outcomes - This is a phrase I coined after
    talking with a lot of roofers about their "why".
    Most don't own a roofing business for the money.
    They do it because that income opens the door
    for adventure, excitement and freedom to do
    what they most want. Others do it for the feeling
    of being able to contribute in large and small
    ways to their communities and to their families.
    An *Ultimate Outcome* is unique, personal, and
    infinitely more powerful than external motivation
    could ever be.

Uniqueness Workshop – This is the name of the
    process we take our clients through that
    permanently eliminates the sameness that exists
    in most roofing contractor marketing. Sameness
    leads to the consumer declaring all contractors
    to be the same and then trying to decide who to
    buy from based on who offers the lowest price.

Glossary of Marketing Terms

Advertising - The act or practice of calling public
    attention to one's product, service, need, etc.,
    especially though paid announcements in

newspapers and magazines, over radio or
television, on billboards, etc.

Bitmap art - Art with filenames ending
in .gif, .bmp, .jpg and .pcx; utilizes pixels that
are saved in a file as a series of numbers; may
become jagged (pixilated) when enlarged

Brand equity - Refers to the marketing effects or
outcomes that improve when a product has a
brand name, compared with those that would
accrue if the same product did not have the
brand name.

Brand loyalty - A consumer's commitment to
repurchase a brand. This can be demonstrated
by repeated buying of a product or service or
other positive behaviors such as word of mouth.

Brand - A kind or variety of something
distinguished by some distinctive characteristic;
a mark made to identify a kind or variety of
something distinguished by some distinctive
characteristic

Branding - In marketing, the sum total of a
company's value, including products, services,
people, advertising, positioning and culture.

Business marketing - The practice of individuals, or
organizations, including commercial businesses,
governments and institutions, facilitating the
sale of their products or services to other

companies or organizations that in turn resell them, use them as components in products or services they offer, or use them to support their operations.

Identity - The condition of being oneself or itself, and not another. The sense of self.

Logo - A graphic representation or symbol of a company name, trademark, abbreviation, etc., often uniquely designed for ready recognition.

Marketing - The promotion of products, especially advertising and branding.

Marketing management – A business discipline focused on the practical application of marketing techniques and the management of a firm's marketing resources and activities.

Marketing mix - Its elements are the basic, tactical components of a marketing plan; price, place, promotion, product.

Marketing strategy – A process that can allow an organization to concentrate its limited resources on the greatest opportunities to increase sales and achieve a sustainable competitive advantage.

Mentor - A wise, influential and trusted counselor or teacher.

Niche marketing – A strategy whereby marketers devote 100% of their efforts towards a small segment of a market instead of the whole market. Niche marketing generally appeals to smaller companies with limited resources.

Positioning - Has come to mean the process by which marketers try to create an image or identity in the minds of their target market for its product, brand, or organization.

Promotional marketing – A business marketing strategy designed to stimulate a customer to take action towards a buying decision.

Promotional Plan - Outlines the promotional tools or tactics you plan to use to accomplish your marketing objectives.

Relationship marketing - Emphasizes customer retention and satisfaction, rather than a dominant focus on "point of sale" transactions.

Strategic marketing - The process of pleasing customers by discovering what they want and making sure you meet their needs.

SWOT analysis - A strategic planning method used to evaluate the Strengths, Weaknesses, Opportunities, and Threats involved in a project or business.

Target market – The segment to which a particular good or service is marketed; mainly defined by age, gender, geography, socio-economic grouping, or any other combination of demographics.

Vector art - Art used by computers (.EPS). Saves images as lines with coordinates of their starting and ending points, and takes up less space on a file; typically used to create business logos and signs.

Acknowledgements

This book, perhaps more so than *80/20 Internet Lead Generation*, needed to be written. You see, in the two years since I was so immersed in the preparation and writing of that first book, I've talked to many, many roofers.

I've asked about your stories.

I've offered to help.

I've gotten help from YOU.

There are stories on both sides of the ledger - those that break your heart and those that make you cheer. Along the way, I've done my best work with a handful of roofing contractors, and it's these men who I want to salute with this project.

Lee, working with you has been inspiring in many ways. Watching your business morph from invisible in search to dominating has been a thrill.

Jon, it's hard to imagine someone accomplishing more than you have in the time we've worked together. Your business has grown and your life has changed for the positive; I'm pleased to have played even a small part in that.

Bill, you in so many ways represent the ideal client relationship for me. Your busy career required you to trust me to do what I said I would do; I'm excited for what we have accomplished during our work together.

While my roofing buddies are the inspiration for this book, such projects are not possible without the smart and skilled eyes and hands of my publisher and team.

Thank you, Warren Whitlock and Corena Golliver, for your contributions to this project.

About the Author

In 2008, after suffering a meltdown in a partnership I was involved with, and, well-prepared after years of working online and generating leads and sales for my own businesses, I launched my own online marketing and internet Lead Generation consulting business.

After working to help motivational speakers succeed online and slowly expanding my client base to include online educators, attorneys, retailers and even plumbers, I landed my first roofing contractor as a client (to visit the website, go to: http://toprankedroofer.com/).

Over the last three years I've helped numerous contractors to achieve their online goals, which makes it possible for them to achieve their Ultimate Outcomes.

In 2014, I published my first book, *80/20 Online Lead Generation*. I've also written eBooks and hundreds of blog posts, and presented at marketing conferences all over the U.S.

My proprietary *Marketplace Domination* method is so powerful, that companies who hire me generate hundreds of targeted, high-quality, exclusive leads from their own website. This allows them to expand and grow their sales and profits exponentially.

Resources

To access the four videos below, along with other bonuses, go to:
http://toprankedroofer.com./bonuses/.

- How To Set-up WordPress on Your Hosting Account

- Completing Basic Keyword Research (Market Samurai)

- Critical Elements of Your Landing Page

- Completing Basic On-page Optimization of your site